A BOOK OI

A BOOK OF BLESSINGS

Compiled and written by
Nick Aiken and Alan Elkins

First published in Great Britain in 2009

Society for Promoting Christian Knowledge
36 Causton Street
London SW1P 4ST

British Library Cataloguing-in-Publication Data
A catalogue record for this book is available from the British Library

ISBN 978–0–281–06099–3

1 3 5 7 9 10 8 6 4 2

Typeset by Graphicraft Ltd, Hong Kong
Printed in Great Britain by Ashford Colour Press

Produced on paper from sustainable forests

Contents

Contents

Acknowledgements

———◦•◦———

We would like to acknowledge the various sources of the blessings that are printed in this book.

- *Promise of His Glory* published jointly by Church House Publishing (Church House, Great Smith Street, London SW1P 3AZ) and Mowbray/Continuum, The Tower Building, 11 York Road, London SE1 7NX.
- *New Parish Prayers* edited by Frank Colquhoun, published by Hodder and Stoughton (338 Euston Road, London NW1 3BH).
- *Pocket Prayers for Peace and Justice* compiled by Christian Aid and published by Church House Publishing (Church House, Great Smith Street, London SW1P 3AZ).
- Extracts taken from *The Iona Abbey Worship Book*, © The Iona Community 2001, published by Wild Goose Publications, Glasgow (<www.ionabooks.com>).
- Extracts from *The Alternative Service Book 1980* (ASB), copyright © the Archbishops' Council and reproduced by permission.
- Extracts from *Common Worship* (CW), copyright © the Archbishops' Council and reproduced by permission.
- Janet Morley, *All Desires Known*, published in 2005 by SPCK (36 Causton Street, London SW1P 4ST).

Scripture quotations are mainly from the Good News Bible, published by The Bible Societies / HarperCollins Publishers Ltd

Acknowledgements

UK © American Bible Society, 1966, 1971, 1976, 1992, 1994; the HOLY BIBLE, NEW INTERNATIONAL VERSION. Copyright © 1973, 1978, 1984 by International Bible Society. Used by permission of Hodder & Stoughton Publishers, a member of the Hachette Livre UK group. All rights reserved. 'NIV' is a registered trademark of International Bible Society. UK trademark number 1448790; and from the Revised Standard Version of the Bible, copyright © 1946, 1952, 1957 and 1971 by the Division of Christian Education of the National Council of the Churches of Christ in the USA. Used by permission. All rights reserved.

We have tried to do a Google search on all of the blessings that we have received and that we have collected over the years. However we have not managed to trace the sources of many of the blessings so the ones which have no name attached to them are ones that we have written or adapted ourselves, or their source is unknown.

Our thanks . . .

We would like to thank the many folk who have kindly contributed to this book either by the blessings that they have written, or over the course of time that they have found from a source which they may have long forgotten. But we would like to thank Giles Williams who offered the bible endings which he had compiled for our book. We would also like to thank John Bundock who contributed 'the blessing of a home' which he wrote some years ago and which was originally available in Guildford Diocese. Additionally our thanks go to George Newton, Bishop Christopher Herbert, Dr Ian Howell, John Fellows, Gill Welford, Bishop Ian Brackley, Elizabeth Burke, Bryony Davis, Richard Fairchild and Edgar Ruddock.

Acknowledgements

A very special thanks also to Carol Sandys who did so much work in arranging this book, typing up material and proof-reading the script. Without her practical and meticulous work this book would never have reached the publisher.

Also our thanks go to Rowan Williams for kindly writing a commendation and supporting this project.

All the royalties from the sale of this book will go to the work of Christian Aid. So we hope that the book will be a blessing to everyone as a valuable resource to those who lead services and to those who are the recipients of the vital work of Christian Aid.

Nick Aiken and Alan Elkins

Introduction

———•◆•———

Welcome to this book. We hope that you enjoy it and find it useful.

Every baptized person is called to be a blessing and to bless others, in word and deed. Within the life of the Church we are called to bless each other and we hope that this book may provide some help towards making our calling a reality.

Some readers may want to write a blessing for a particular occasion, so here is how to go about it in a traditional way.

Writing a blessing requires that we understand the basic structure so that we can follow it, or, if needs be, know that we are departing from the structure, as many modern blessings do.

As an example we might look at a well-known blessing:

> The peace of God,
> which passes all understanding,
> keep your hearts and minds
> in the knowledge and love of God,
> and of his Son Jesus Christ our Lord,
> and the blessing of God almighty,
> the Father, the Son, and the Holy Spirit,
> be among you and remain with you always.
> Amen.
>
> (*Common Worship*)

First of all there is a statement about the nature or property of God:

> The peace of God,
> which passes all understanding,

This is followed by something we want God to do for us or others:

> keep your hearts and minds
> in the knowledge and love of God,
> and of his Son Jesus Christ our Lord,

The whole is rounded off with a formal declaration of blessing:

> and the blessing of God almighty,
> the Father, the Son, and the Holy Spirit,
> be among you and remain with you always.
> Amen.

So – to take a hypothetical example – the blessing of a newly refurbished lounge in a home for the elderly portrays a process of development:

opening statement:

> Ever caressing God

a connecting line:

> we give you thanks for the skill of those who worked to
> refurbish this room

what we want God to do:

> may your people here find rest,
> refreshment for their bodies
> and peace for their souls

a declaration:

> and the blessing of God,
> who is Father, Son and Holy Spirit,
> be among those who rest here now and always.
> Amen.

So we have:

> Ever caressing God,
> we give you thanks for the skill of those who worked to
>   refurbish this room.
> May your people here find rest;
> refreshment for their bodies,
> and peace for their souls;
> and the blessing of God,
> who is Father, Son and Holy Spirit,
> be among those who rest here now and always.
> Amen.

Then read it to yourself *out loud* to hear if there is anything which does not scan and adjust, if necessary, and add or change punctuation, as in the final version above.

A final thought: we generally do not bless objects for the sake of the objects themselves. Rather we bless the people who will use the objects or the use to which the objects will be put.

Alan Elkins

SEASONS

Advent

Christ the Sun of Righteousness shine upon you, scatter the darkness from before your path, and make you ready to meet him when he comes in glory; and the blessing of God, Father, Son and Holy Spirit, be among you and remain with you always. Amen.

May the Lord watch over you, as you grow in faith and love. May your lives be filled with kindness and joy. And the blessing of God, Father, Son and Holy Spirit, be among you, and remain with you always. Amen.

May the Lord bless you with his peace, sustain you with his mercy and enrich you with his presence throughout the coming week, and the blessing of God, Father, Son and Holy Spirit, be upon you, now and always. Amen.

May the love of Christ be born in us.
May our eyes be open to see him in others.
May we always have hope.
And may God bless us,
Father, Son and Holy Spirit. Amen.

May God give us the courage to receive him.
May we greet him with joy.
May we carry him in our hearts to others.
And the blessing of God, Father, Son and Holy Spirit, be
    with us all. Amen.

3

May the Lord be generous in increasing your love.
May the Lord confirm your hearts in holiness.
And the blessing of God, the Father, the Son and the Holy
    Spirit, be among you, and remain with you always. Amen.

May the Father bless you as his children.
May the Son acknowledge you as his disciples.
May the Spirit guide you in your ways.
And the blessing of God, Father, Son and Holy Spirit, be upon
    you always. Amen.

May God the Father, who loved the world so much that he
    sent his only Son,
give you grace to prepare for life eternal. Amen.
May God the Son, who comes to us as Redeemer and Judge,
reveal to you the path from darkness to light.
May God the Holy Spirit, by whose working the Virgin Mary
    conceived the Christ,
help you bear the fruits of holiness. Amen.
And the blessing of God Almighty,
the Father, the Son, and the Holy Spirit,
be upon you and remain with you always. Amen.

                                    (*Promise of His Glory*)

May God the Father, Judge all-merciful,
make us worthy of a place in his kingdom. Amen.
May God the Son, coming among us in power,
reveal in our midst the promise of his glory. Amen.
May God the Holy Spirit make us steadfast in faith,
joyful in hope and constant in love. Amen.
And the blessing of God Almighty,

the Father, the Son, and the Holy Spirit,
be upon you and remain with you always. Amen.

(*Promise of His Glory*)

May God himself, the God of peace,
make you perfect and holy;
and keep you safe and blameless, in spirit, soul and body,
for the coming of our Lord Jesus Christ;
and the blessing of God Almighty,
the Father, the Son, and the Holy Spirit,
be upon you and remain with you always. Amen.

(*Promise of His Glory*)

Christmas

May the Lord bless your life with simplicity and peace,
may your homes be full of life and joy.
And the blessing of God, the Father, Son and Holy Spirit,
   be among you, and remain with you always. Amen.

May the grace of the Lord be your strength.
May the truth of the Lord be your guide.
May the love of the Lord be your salvation.
And the blessing of God, Father, Son and Holy Spirit,
   be among you, and remain with you always. Amen.

May your families and your communities be blessed with the
   spirit of the home at Nazareth.
And the blessing of God, Father, Son and Holy Spirit,
   be among you, and remain with you always. Amen.

May the Lord give you light and understanding.
May the Lord give you wisdom and grace.
May the blessing of God, Father, Son and Holy Spirit,
   be among you, and remain with you always. Amen.

May God give you the grace to hear his calling, and to follow
him in love and obedience; and the blessing of God, Father,
Son and Holy Spirit, be upon you and remain with you always.
Amen.

Christ, who by his incarnation gathered into one things earthly and heavenly, fill you with peace and goodwill and make you partakers of the divine nature; and the blessing of God, Father, Son and Holy Spirit, be among you and remain with you always. Amen.

May the grace of the Lord Jesus, born as one of us, fill your
  lives with his love,
fill your hearts with his peace,
and clothe you now in his righteousness;
and the blessing of God, Father, Son and Holy Spirit, be upon
  you now and always. Amen.

May the joy of the angels,
the eagerness of the shepherds,
the perseverance of the wise men,
the obedience of Joseph and Mary,
and the peace of the Christ Child
be yours this Christmas
and the blessing of God Almighty, the Father, the Son,
  and the Holy Spirit,
be upon you and remain with you always.
Amen.

(*Promise of His Glory*)

Epiphany

May the God of all consolation, who leads us with a shepherd's care, hold you close in his arms and bless you. And the blessing of God, the Father, Son and Holy Spirit, be among you, and remain with you always. Amen.

Christ the Son of God perfect in you the image of his glory and gladden your hearts with the good news of his kingdom; and the blessing of God, Father, Son and Holy Spirit, be among you and remain with you always. Amen.

May God who accepted Abram's offering accept our offering.
May Jesus who attended a wedding in Cana attend our hearts
and homes.
May the Spirit who enlightens us fill our minds with truth.
And the blessing of God, Father, Son and Holy Spirit, be with
you always. Amen.

May God fill you with his life and hope.
May he strengthen you in mind and body.
And the blessing of God be with you, now and always. Amen.

May God's love and mercy be always with you.
May Christ lead you into the joy of the kingdom.
May the Spirit deepen your faith, hope and love.
And may God bless you, Father, Son and Holy Spirit. Amen.

May the Lord protect you and keep you.
May he send his peace upon you.
And the blessing of God, the Father, Son and Holy Spirit,
 be among you, and remain with you always. Amen.

May the Lord inspire you and fill your lives with brightness
 and truth.
May the guiding star of Bethlehem direct and comfort you.
And the blessing of God, the Father, Son and Holy Spirit,
 be among you, and remain with you always. Amen.

Naming of Jesus

May the three-personed God, who called you into being, lead
you ever deeper into the mystery of his creative and redemptive
love. And the blessing of God, Father, Son and Holy Spirit, be
upon you and remain with you always. Amen.

Baptism of Christ

The Holy Spirit has come upon you and you have been
anointed with the joy of Christ. May the good news of salvation, in all its richness, find a home in your hearts; and may the
blessing of God, Father, Son and Holy Spirit, come down upon
you and remain with you for ever. Amen.

May the Lord show you his face.
May he transfigure your life.
May he bring you to glory.
And the blessing of God, Father, Son and Holy Spirit,
 be upon you always. Amen.

May the God of heaven and earth strengthen you.
May his love comfort you.
May he protect you and give you peace.
And the blessing of God, Father, Son and Holy Spirit,
    be upon you always. Amen.

May the God who loves you turn his face towards you.
May you reflect the beauty of his countenance to all you meet.
May your hearts overflow with the love and confidence of
    his presence within you;
and the blessing of God, Father, Son and Holy Spirit, be upon
    you always. Amen.

May you always be able to lift your eyes to a future with God.
May you walk with confidence and with pride in this hope.
May the Holy Spirit keep you safe.
And the blessing of God, Father, Son and Holy Spirit,
    be upon you always. Amen.

Presentation of Christ

Christ who has nourished us with himself the living bread,
make you one in praise and love, and raise you up at the last
day; and the blessing of God, who is Father, Son and Holy
Spirit, be with you always. Amen.

(ASB)

May you always be conscious of God's love for you.
May you experience his healing when you are hurt.
May you know his presence when you are alone;
and the blessing of God, Father, Son and Holy Spirit, always
    remain with you. Amen.

Go out into the world knowing you are the beloved children of our loving heavenly Father. And may the example of Christ and the power of his Spirit enable you to reflect the Father's love to those you meet this week; and the blessing of God, Father, Son and Holy Spirit, be among you and remain with you always. Amen.

Christ the Son of God, born of Mary, fill you with his grace to trust his promises and obey his will; and the blessing of God, Father, Son and Holy Spirit, be upon you always. Amen.

(ASB)

Lent and Passiontide

——•◆•——

Ash Wednesday

May God's grace reconcile us to Christ; may Christ's love reconcile us to the Father; and may the indwelling presence of the Holy Spirit reconcile us to one another; and the blessing of God, Father, Son and Holy Spirit, be among you and remain with you always. Amen.

Christ crucified draw you to himself, to find in him a sure ground for faith, a firm support for hope, and the assurance of sins forgiven; and the blessing of God, Father, Son and Holy Spirit, be among you and remain with you always. Amen.

(ASB)

Christ give you grace to grow in holiness, to deny yourselves, take up your cross, and follow him; and the blessing of God, Father, Son and Holy Spirit, be among you and remain with you always. Amen.

(ASB)

May he whose word spoke and everything began, speak to our hearts.
May the Word which became flesh be with us in our lives.
May the Lord, our Comforter, direct our hearts and minds.
And the blessing of God, Father, Son and Holy Spirit, be with us now and always. Amen.

13

May God the Father grant you a vision of his glory;
the Son enlighten you by the brightness of his face;
and the Holy Spirit fill you with power to live the good news.
And the blessing of God, Father, Son and Holy Spirit, be upon
   you, now and always. Amen.

May the Lord fill your lives with peace,
may the Lord fill your hearts with love,
may the Lord fill your mind with light;
and may the Lord bless you, Father, Son and Holy Spirit.
   Amen.

May the cross of Christ be our glory.
May the limitless love of God be our security.
May the wisdom of the Spirit be our guide;
and the blessing of God, Father, Son and Holy Spirit, be upon
   us now and for ever. Amen.

Go in peace, and may God's arms surround you and embrace
you, and may the Holy Spirit fill your hearts with truth, beauty
and love, and may Christ Jesus our Lord walk with you and
guide your every step both now and for evermore. Amen.

Lent and Passiontide

May Christ, our Living Lord, who was betrayed, denied, and
   who suffered for us, be with us in our lives this week.
May he be welcome in our homes and in our hearts;
and the blessing of God, Father, Son and Holy Spirit, be
   among us, and remain with us always. Amen.

Saving God,
you gave wise men a glorious star to lead them to Christ;
lead us ever onward towards him;
so may the blessing of God, Father, Son and Holy Spirit,
be upon us and remain with us,
now and for ever. Amen.

Loving God,
as your Son lived in obedience to you,
make us watchful for your will;
so may the blessing of God, Father, Son and Holy Spirit,
be upon us and remain with us,
now and for ever. Amen.

Lord Jesus, you gave up all to be one with us:
include us in your circle of love;
so may the blessing of God, Father, Son and Holy Spirit,
be upon us and remain with us,
now and for ever. Amen.

Lord God, you call us to live as Christians:
enable us to choose the good and refuse evil;
so may the blessing of God, Father, Son and Holy Spirit,
be upon us and remain with us,
now and for ever. Amen.

Ever caressing God,
by the cross your Son drew all peoples to himself:
draw us similarly close;
so may the blessing of God, Father, Son and Holy Spirit,
be upon us and remain with us,
now and for ever. Amen.

15

Lord, and Saviour God,
nails could not hold your Son to the Cross:
free us to live his risen life;
so may the blessing of God, Father, Son and Holy Spirit,
be upon us and remain with us,
now and for ever. Amen.

Ever loving God,
by the birth of your Son you made us one with you;
bless us in our lives and make us a blessing to others
for the glory of your Son, Jesus the Christ. Amen.

Lord Jesus Christ, the cross conceals your glory:
imprint on our hearts that same hidden glory;
so may the blessing of God, Father, Son and Holy Spirit,
be upon us and remain with us,
now and for ever. Amen.

Lord Jesus Christ,
you hold our hearts in yours:
transform and help us to grow;
so may the blessing of God, Father, Son and Holy Spirit,
be upon us and remain with us,
now and for ever. Amen.

O Lord our God, at our baptism you sealed us
with the sign of the Cross:
make us mindful of your presence in our lives;
so may the blessing of God, Father, Son and Holy Spirit,
be upon us and remain with us,
now and for ever. Amen.

O Lord Jesus Christ, by your Passion you opened the doors of
    an infinite mercy:
give us gifts of repentance and pardon;
so may the blessing of God, Father, Son and Holy Spirit,
be upon us and remain with us,
now and for ever. Amen.

Loving God, when hands that had fashioned the earth washed
    disciples' feet
you showed the nature of kingship:
so make us serve for your sake;
and may the blessing of God, Father, Son and Holy Spirit,
be upon us and remain with us,
now and for ever. Amen.

Give us, O God, this day, and always, to keep the great
    commandment of love;
so may the blessing of God, Father, Son and Holy Spirit,
be upon us and remain with us,
now and for ever. Amen.

Lord Jesus Christ, our great High Priest,
enable us to offer our lives in service;
so may the blessing of God, Father, Son and Holy Spirit,
be upon us and remain with us,
now and for ever. Amen.

Loving God, community of love,
bind us together in bonds of love and affection;
so may the blessing of God, who is Father, Son and Holy
    Spirit,
be upon us and remain with us,
now and for ever. Amen.

Master and Lord,
set your law plainly within our hearts
that we may serve you;
so may the blessing of God, Father, Son and Holy Spirit,
be upon us and remain with us,
now and for ever. Amen.

Loving God,
give us the strength to stay with you when times are hard;
so may the blessing of God, Father, Son and Holy Spirit,
be upon us and remain with us,
now and for ever. Amen.

Ever caring God,
your Son was often betrayed,
keep us loyal and make us faithful;
so may the blessing of God, Father, Son and Holy Spirit,
be upon us and remain with us,
now and for ever. Amen.

O Lord, our Redeemer and King,
consecrate our minds to the ministry of truth;
so may the blessing of God, Father, Son and Holy Spirit,
be upon us and remain with us,
now and for ever. Amen.

Lord God of truth,
give us the strength to be truth-makers;
so may the blessing of God, Father, Son and Holy Spirit,
be upon us and remain with us,
now and for ever. Amen.

God give you strength to take up your cross as you follow
    Christ;
so may the blessing of God, Father, Son and Holy Spirit,
be upon you and remain with you,
now and for ever. Amen.

God, your Son, Jesus the Christ, was poor for our sake:
give us a spirit of poverty and service;
so may the blessing of God, Father, Son and Holy Spirit,
be upon us and remain with us,
now and for ever. Amen.

Ever loving God, your Son was raised on the throne of the
    cross:
reign in our hearts to your glory;
so may the blessing of God, Father, Son and Holy Spirit,
be upon us and remain with us,
now and for ever. Amen.

Lord God, your Son reigns from the cross:
give us a spirit of service as a symbol of our power;
so may the blessing of God, Father, Son and Holy Spirit,
be upon us and remain with us,
now and for ever. Amen.

Lord God, help us to gaze upon your Son
and see in him the openings of your love for us;
so may the blessing of God, Father, Son and Holy Spirit,
be upon us and remain with us,
now and for ever. Amen.

Palm Sunday

Christ crucified draw you to himself,
to find in him a sure ground for faith,
a firm support for hope,
and the assurance of sins forgiven;
and the blessing of God, Father, Son and Holy Spirit,
be among you and remain with you always. Amen.

(CW)

May God be with you in all the events of your daily living.
May he help you to understand that hurt and failure play their
   part in our redemption.
And may the Father, Son and Holy Spirit bless you now and
   always. Amen.

Holy Week

May God the Father, who sent his Son into the world to take
   on our human form,
give you a knowledge and understanding of his infinite
   love.
May God the Son, who was obedient even to torture and
   death on a cross,
give you an awareness of his eternal grace and presence.
May God the Holy Spirit, who came unseen as the wind,
give you the inner strength to live as a child of God and a life
   of obedience to his call;
and the blessing of God, Father, Son and Holy Spirit, be upon
   you and remain with you always.

Maundy Thursday

May our Lord Jesus, the Christ, wash your feet, then guide them to dance for him. And the blessing of God, Father, Son and Holy Spirit, be with you now, and remain with you always. Amen.

You are disciples of the Lord: live in his love.
You are messengers of the Lord: deliver his love;
and the blessing of God, Father, Son and Holy Spirit,
    be among you, and remain with you always. Amen.

Easter

May the risen Christ fill you with hope.
May the risen Christ give you joy.
May the risen Christ bring you healing and peace.
May God bless you, Father, Son and Holy Spirit. Amen.

The God of peace,
who brought again from the dead our Lord Jesus,
that great shepherd of the sheep,
through the blood of the eternal covenant,
make you perfect in every good work to do his will,
working in you that which is well-pleasing in his sight;
and the blessing of God, Father, Son and Holy Spirit,
be among you and remain with you always. Amen.

(CW)

May the Good Shepherd lead you into all truth.
May the Good Shepherd guard you from danger.
May the Good Shepherd bring you to your everlasting home.
May God bless you, Father, Son and Holy Spirit. Amen.

Merciful Father, you gave your Son Jesus, the Christ, to be
the good shepherd, and in his love for us to lay down his life
and rise again: keep us always under his protection, and give us
grace to follow in his steps; and may his blessing be upon us
and remain with us always. Amen.

Jesus is the Way, the Truth and the Light. May you walk in his paths, know his truth and be bathed in his light. And the blessing of God, Father, Son and Holy Spirit, be with you in your pilgrimage. Amen.

The Spirit of truth lead you into all truth, give you grace to confess that Jesus Christ is Lord, and strengthen you to proclaim the word and works of God; and the blessing of God, Father, Son and Holy Spirit, be among you and remain with you always. Amen.

(ASB)

May the peace of the loving God be with you;
May the love of the risen Lord Jesus embrace you;
May the power of the Holy Spirit uphold you and inspire you,
and the blessing of God, Father, Son and Holy Spirit, be upon
　　you always. Amen.

May Christ's face shed its light upon you.
May you come to know his goodness.
May your lives be transformed by his peace.
And the blessing of God, Father, Son and Holy Spirit, be upon
　　you always. Amen.

May those who are hungry be fed from the tree of life.
May those who are thirsty be refreshed by the water of life.
And the blessing of God, Father, Son and Holy Spirit, be upon
　　you always. Amen.

May you be guided by the voice of the shepherd.
May you be strengthened by the love of the shepherd.
May your lives be blessed by the goodness of the shepherd.

And the blessing of God, Father, Son and Holy Spirit,
  be among you, and remain with you always. Amen.

May you pass your days in the knowledge of God's promises.
May you find reassurance in the Word of Life.
May you live every day in the joy of this Easter Day.
And the blessing of God, Father, Son and Holy Spirit, be with
  you today and always. Amen.

May the Father's love for you have no end.
May the Son grant you salvation.
May the Spirit breathe life into you.
And the blessing of God, Father, Son and Holy Spirit, be with
  you always. Amen.

May the Lord show his face to you.
May he feed you and give you his power.
May the Lord walk with you wherever you go.
And the blessing of God, Father, Son and Holy Spirit,
  be among you, now and always. Amen.

May the Father shower his love upon you.
May the Son strengthen you in your faith.
May the Spirit breathe his life afresh in you and give you
  peace.
And may God bless you, Father, Son and Holy Spirit. Amen.

May you feel the compassion of Christ in your life.
May he give you his strength to do his will.
May you feel safe in his arms.
And the blessing of God, Father, Son and Holy Spirit,
  be among you, and remain with you always. Amen.

May you be strengthened through the bread of life.
May you be made more whole through the word of life.
May you become wise through the light of life.
And the blessing of God, Father, Son and Holy Spirit,
    be among you, and remain with you always. Amen.

May God mould you in his way of love.
May Jesus guide you with his teaching.
May the Holy Spirit protect and empower you.
And may you be blessed by the Father, Son and Holy Spirit all
    the days of your life. Amen.

May you receive the word of the Lord with faith.
May you taste the living bread.
May you be nourished by the waters of life.
And the blessing of God be with you always, Father, Son and
    Holy Spirit. Amen.

May God always hear your prayers and answer.
May the Living Bread always sustain you.
May the Spirit fill you with joy and hope.
And may God, Father, Son and Holy Spirit, bless you and
    those you love. Amen.

May the Father draw you to himself in his Covenant of love.
May the Son feed you with the bread of life.
May the Spirit inspire you to live in openness and peace.
And the blessing of God be with you, Father, Son and Holy
    Spirit. Amen.

May God bring us to the knowledge of his will.
May he teach us to keep his law and honour his commands.

May he guide us always in the ways of truth and integrity.
And the blessing of God, Father, Son and Holy Spirit, be upon
you and remain with you always. Amen.

May the Father open our ears to his wisdom.
May the Son open our eyes to his light.
May the Spirit enliven us with the gift of love.
And the blessing of God, Father, Son and Holy Spirit, be with
us now and always. Amen.

May the Lord free you from everything that weighs you down.
May he seal you with his Spirit as the promise of salvation.
And the blessing of God, Father, Son and Holy Spirit,
be among you, and remain with you always. Amen.

May you experience the love of the Father every day.
May you know the compassion of Christ every day.
May you be empowered with the strength of the Spirit every
day.
And may the blessing of God, Father, Son and Holy Spirit,
be with you, your whole life long. Amen.

May the Father's gentle call bring you to his side.
May the voice of Jesus draw you into the circle of his loving
arms.
May the Holy Spirit fill you with wisdom and courage to be
free.
And the blessing of God, Father, Son and Holy Spirit, be with
you in all your ways. Amen.

May the Father strengthen and confirm your faith in him.
May the Son heal you and bring you his peace.

May the Spirit of love cast out darkness from your hearts.
May the Father, the Son and the Holy Spirit bless you, both
    now and always. Amen.

May God who is your Creator, Saviour and Protector, keep you
from all harm, fill you with his love and lead you safely to his
Kingdom; and may God, Father, Son and Holy Spirit, bless you
and keep you. Amen.

May God the Holy Spirit lead you into the holiness and light of
God's kingdom. And the blessing of God, Father, Son and Holy
Spirit, be upon you now and always. Amen.

May the Lord show you mercy.
May the Lord grant you peace.
May the Lord bring you joy.
And the blessing of God, Father, Son and Holy Spirit,
    be among you, and remain with you always. Amen.

May God our Father hold you each day in his love.
May Christ who died and rose again give you hope.
May the Spirit empower you to come through all suffering.
May God, Father, Son and Holy Spirit, bless you always.
    Amen.

Ascension

May the God, who made you, watch over you.
May the Lord, who died for you, be near you.
May the Spirit, who gives life, live in your hearts.
And the blessing of this all-holy God,
the Father, Son and Holy Spirit, be with you always. Amen.

May the Father show you his salvation.
May the Son come to dwell in your hearts.
May the Spirit keep you in love.
And the blessing of God, Father, Son and Holy Spirit, be upon
you always. Amen.

Christ our ascended King pour upon you the abundance of
his gifts and bring you to reign with him in glory; and the blessing of God, the Father, Son and Holy Spirit, be among you and
remain with you always. Amen.

(CW)

May the Lord constantly hover over you as you travel.
May the Lord brighten your path every step of the way.
May the Lord fill you with his grace and keep you faithful and
strong through your journey of life.
And the blessing of God, Father, Son and Holy Spirit, be with
you always. Amen.

May you always know the depth of God's love for you.
May you give whatever you have into his care.

29

May you always feel his blessing upon you.
And the blessing of God, Father, Son and Holy Spirit, be with
you today and always. Amen.

May the love of God enfold you, the peace of God fill your
hearts, and the blessing of the loving God be upon you now
and always. Amen.

May the Lord grant you wisdom to know his will, to follow his
way and to remain in his love. And the blessing of God come
down upon you and remain with you always, Father, Son and
Holy Spirit. Amen.

Pentecost

The Spirit of truth lead you into all truth,
give you grace to confess that Jesus Christ is Lord,
and strengthen you to proclaim the word and works of God;
and the blessing of God, Father, Son and Holy Spirit,
be among you, and remain with you always. Amen.

(CW)

May God the Father fill you with his strength.
May God the Son fill you with his peace.
May God the Holy Spirit fill you with his presence.
And the blessing of God, Father, Son and Holy Spirit,
be among you, and remain with you always. Amen.

May the Father's mercy touch you,
The Son's peace fill you,
And the Spirit's presence stay with you.
And the blessing of God, Father, Son and Holy Spirit,
be among you, and remain with you always. Amen.

May God the Father fill you with his grace,
God the Son fill you with his love,
God the Holy Spirit fill you with his peace.
And the blessing of God, Father, Son and Holy Spirit,
be among you, and remain with you always. Amen.

May God give you strength.
May God give you hope.

May God give you joy.
And the blessing of God, Father, Son and Holy Spirit,
 be among you, and remain with you always. Amen.

May peace dwell in your heart.
May peace fill your home.
May peace be yours always.
And the blessing of God, Father, Son and Holy Spirit,
 be among you, and remain with you always. Amen.

May the God who listens to the prayer of the poor, and the cry of the needy, bless you with his love. And the blessing of God, Father, Son and Holy Spirit, be among you, and remain with you always. Amen.

May the Lord of all kindliness enkindle in you the fire of his love, and make of you a welcoming people. And the blessing of God, Father, Son and Holy Spirit, be among you, and remain with you always. Amen.

May God be the focus of your searching.
May you find him in each moment of your days.
May the abundance of his love overwhelm you.
And may God bless you, Father, Son and Holy Spirit. Amen.

God preserve you in the wealth of his love.
Christ preserve you in the riches of his grace.
The Holy Spirit preserve you in the fullness of wisdom.
And the blessing of God, Father, Son and Holy Spirit, be with
 you always. Amen.

May the Lord inspire your thoughts, accompany your deeds and preserve your real treasure. And the blessing of God, Father,

Son and Holy Spirit, be among you, and remain with you
always. Amen.

May the Lord lead you on your journey through life.
May he give you courage to do always what is right.
And the blessing of God, Father, Son and Holy Spirit,
   be among you, and remain with you always. Amen.

May you be sure of God's love for you,
certain of Christ's care for you,
and may you be assured of the Spirit's presence with you;
and the blessing of God, Father, Son and Holy Spirit,
   be among you, and remain with you always. Amen.

May the God of all gentleness and compassion be always with
   you.
May he give you courage and strength.
May he fill you with his Spirit of love and peace.
And the blessing of God, Father, Son and Holy Spirit,
   be among you, and remain with you always. Amen.

May the Lord grant us true freedom,
and true strength to take up our cross and follow him,
and may the Lord favour us with the happiness of true
   discipleship;
and the blessing of God, Father, Son and Holy Spirit,
   be among us, and remain with us always. Amen.

May the love of God which was in Christ Jesus, be your hope
   and your joy.
May God's compassion bring you peace.
May God's will become your will.

And the blessing of God, Father, Son and Holy Spirit,
    be among you, and remain with you always. Amen.

God has called us out of darkness into light.
May he fill you with his light and hope and keep you free
    from all anxiety;
and the blessing of God, Father, Son and Holy Spirit,
    be among you, and remain with you always. Amen.

May God grant you the courage to speak out for truth and
    justice,
the wisdom to know what to say,
and the strength to put your words into practice;
and the blessing of God, Father, Son and Holy Spirit,
    be among you, and remain with you always. Amen.

Now may the Lord of peace himself give you peace at all times
and in every way. The Lord be with you all; and the blessing of
God, Father, Son and Holy Spirit, be among you, and remain
with you always. Amen.

May God fill you with the Pentecostal fire of his love, to change
your hearts and lives in the transforming power of his Spirit.
And may his blessing be upon you, Father, Son and Holy Spirit.
Amen.

Trinity

God the Holy Trinity make you strong in faith and love, defend you on every side, and guide you in truth and peace; and the blessing of God, the Father, the Son, and the Holy Spirit, be among you and remain with you always. Amen.

(CW)

May God be the beginning and end of your story.
May Christ be the centre and foundation of your story.
May the Spirit be the spark that brings your story to life.
May God bless you, Father, Son and Holy Spirit. Amen.

The Lord give you ears to hear his call, a heart to respond to his love, and a tongue to tell of the wonders he has done; and the blessing of God, Father, Son and Holy Spirit, be upon you always. Amen.

May the Father remove all your sadness.
May the Son fill you with joy.
May the Holy Spirit lead you safely to God's home.
And may God bless you, the Father, the Son, and the Holy
    Spirit. Amen.

May you welcome the Lord at all times.
May you witness to Christ without fear.
May you call on the Spirit for wisdom and strength.
And may God bless you, Father, Son and Holy Spirit. Amen.

May the Father lead you to his kingdom.
May the Son gift you with peace.
May the Spirit overwhelm your hearts with love.
And the blessing of God, Father, Son and Holy Spirit, be upon
you always. Amen.

May the God who listens to the prayer of the poor, and the cry
of the needy, bless you with his love. And the blessing of God,
Father, Son and Holy Spirit, be upon you always. Amen.

The Lord give you wisdom and discernment.
The Lord give you joy and hope.
The Lord give you a hunger for justice and a thirst for peace.
And the blessing of God, Father, Son and Holy Spirit, be upon
you always. Amen.

May God the Father of our Lord Jesus, the Christ, who is the
source of all goodness and growth, pour his blessing upon all
things created, and upon you his children, that you may use
them to his glory and the welfare of all peoples. And the blessing of God, Father, Son and Holy Spirit, be upon you always.
Amen.

May Christ, who walked on the waters, be your salvation.
May he give you light in darkness.
May he be at your side always.
And may the blessing of God, Father, Son and Holy Spirit,
be with you now and for ever. Amen.

May the mercy of God dawn upon us.
May the justice of God reign among us.

Trinity

May the wisdom of God guide our lives;
and the blessing of God, Father, Son and Holy Spirit, be upon
us always. Amen.

May God give you peace.
May God show you love.
May God bring you to glory.
And the blessing of God, Father, Son and Holy Spirit, be upon
you always. Amen.

May you be filled with strength and confidence in following
the path of Christ.
May God's love and mercy fill you with hope and courage.
And the blessing of God, the Father, Son and Holy Spirit,
be with you always. Amen.

May the God of justice and compassion fill your life with his
goodness and love.
May he give you peace and strength, and bless you, the Father,
the Son, and the Holy Spirit. Amen.

May God show you mercy and fill you with grace.
May God give you peace and a vision of glory.
May God move your hearts to forgive and to love.
May God bless you, the Father, Son and Holy Spirit. Amen.

May you always be aware of God's great love for you.
May that love for you live in your hearts.
May it show forth in your actions.
And the blessing of God, Father, Son and Holy Spirit,
be among you now and for ever. Amen.

May the Lord who is just, keep you in his truth.
May the Lord who is tender-hearted, show you his love.
And may you all grow with the blessing of God upon you;
the blessing of God, the Father, Son and Holy Spirit. Amen.

May you be filled with compassion and understanding.
May you be strengthened and filled with new life.
May you be guided in the truth.
And the blessing of God, Father, Son and Holy Spirit, be with
you now and always. Amen.

May the Lord watch over and bless all who suffer.
May Jesus strengthen those he calls to service.
May the Spirit inspire us all to action beyond our imagining.
And the blessing of God, Father, Son and Holy Spirit, rest
upon us. Amen.

May you come to know the one, true God.
May you bless the name of the Lord for ever.
May you live in the love of God.
And the blessing of God, Father, Son and Holy Spirit,
be among you, now and always. Amen.

MINOR SEASONAL EVENTS

Mothering Sunday

Loving God, as a mother feeds her children at the breast, you feed us in this sacrament with the food and drink of eternal life; help us who have tasted your goodness to grow in grace within the household of faith; and may you fill us with the fullness of your blessing, now and evermore. Amen.

May the Lord bless you and keep you safe.
May the Lord watch over you and protect you.
And the blessing of God, Father, Son and Holy Spirit, be upon
 you always. Amen.

May God the Holy Trinity, Family Divine, hold you in safe keeping and grant you love and joy and peace. And the blessing of God be with you, Father, Son and Holy Spirit. Amen.

May the God of all kindness and truth inspire you to live in honesty and affection for each other. And may God bless you this day, the Father, the Son, and the Holy Spirit. Amen.

May you always know the love of God for you.
May you have the courage to put his ways above all others.
And may you always be blessed with the blessing of the
 Father, Son and Holy Spirit. Amen.

May God give you fresh hope today.
May you be filled with courage and strengthened by his
 power.

May you enter fully into this season of Lent and be filled with
the joy of Easter.
And the blessing of God, Father, Son and Holy Spirit, be with
you, now and always. Amen.

May God create within us new birth and fresh vision.
May Jesus, our Saviour, accompany us.
May God, the Holy Spirit, inspire us to long for God's grace.
And the blessing of God, Father, Son and Holy Spirit, be upon
you always. Amen.

May God pour the waters of his love upon our dryness.
May we never tire of loving him.
May we always reach out to others in need.
And the blessing of God, Father, Son and Holy Spirit, be upon
you always. Amen.

May you come out of the darkness of doubt and disbelief into
the certainty of God's love. May the blessing of God, full of compassion and of love, come down upon you and be always with
you, the Father, Son and Holy Spirit. Amen.

May the Father's love be your guide and strength in all your days.
May Jesus' teaching be your example throughout your life.
May the Spirit be your inspiration to love without ceasing.
And the blessing of God, Father, Son and Holy Spirit,
    be among you, and remain with you always. Amen.

May you know God's welcome in each new day's morning.
May you know Christ's peace in the busyness of noonday.
May the Spirit be with you all your days.
And the blessing of God, Father, Son and Holy Spirit,
    be among you, and remain with you always. Amen.

Transfiguration

May the Lord forgive what you have been, sanctify what you are, and direct what you will be; and the blessing of God, Father, Son and Holy Spirit, be upon you and those whom you love, now and always. Amen.

May God the Father, whose immeasurable glory shone forth in his Son Jesus, the Christ, transform your own hearts and minds by the power of his Holy Spirit; and the blessing of God, Father, Son and Holy Spirit be with you now and always. Amen.

May you always be conscious of God's love for you.
May you experience his healing when you are hurt.
May you know his presence when you are alone.
And may the blessing of God always be upon you, Father,
    Son and Holy Spirit. Amen.

May the peace of Christ overcome your anxieties.
May your hearts remain open to his call.
May the Spirit fill you with his love.
May God, Father, Son and Holy Spirit, bless you. Amen.

May the re-creating grace of Christ reassure us.
May the forgiveness of God's love heal us.
May the power of the Holy Spirit dwell within us;
and the blessing of God, Father, Son and Holy Spirit, be ever
    upon us. Amen.

May the Father unfold to you his wisdom.
May the Son make you alive to his glory.
May the Spirit live with love in your hearts.
And may God bless you, Father, Son and Holy Spirit. Amen.

May the scales be lifted from our eyes, that we may truly see.
May the shadows be lifted from our hearts, that we may really
    love.
May the wisdom of God grow in our minds, that we may
    follow him for ever.
And may God bless us, Father, Son and Holy Spirit, today and
    always. Amen.

The God of all grace, who called you to his eternal glory in
Christ Jesus, establish, strengthen and settle you in the faith.
And the blessing of God, Father, Son and Holy Spirit, be upon
you this day and through all the days that are to come. Amen.

In your doubting may God's truth become clear to you.
In your fear may the hand of God be open to hold you.
In your darkness may God's light become your new dawn.
And may God bless you, Father, Son and Holy Spirit. Amen.

Harvest

May God the Father bless you, who first sowed the seed of
   eternal life in your hearts;
may God the Son bless you, who nurtures you with the rain
   and sunshine of love;
may God the Spirit bless you, who brings us all to fruition;
and may the blessing of God be among you and remain with
   you always. Amen.

May God our provider make you faithful and strong to do his
will, that you may reign with him in glory; and the blessing of
God, Father, Son and Holy Spirit, be among you, and remain
with you always. Amen.

May the Spirit of hope and light strengthen you, give you
   peace and be with you always.
May the Good Shepherd guide you and keep you safe.
And the blessing of God, Father, Son and Holy Spirit,
   be among you, and remain with you always. Amen.

May God grant you the wisdom to choose the fullness of life.
May Christ inspire you to serve the world.
May the Holy Spirit empower and strengthen your faith in
   action.
And may the blessing of God be with you always, Father, Son
   and Holy Spirit. Amen.

All Souls

May God bring you his comfort, his peace, his courage and his hope both today and in the days to come. And the blessing of God, Father, Son and Holy Spirit, be upon you now and always. Amen.

We give thanks for all those who have gone before us and who have meant so much to us during their lives. So may we be inspired to follow their good examples of faith and love. And may the blessing of God, sustainer and provider, be with us each day. Amen.

May the Holy Spirit, who gives comfort and strength, Jesus Christ, who gives hope and life, and God the Father, who gives meaning and purpose, touch and bless your lives today and everyday from this time forth and for evermore. Amen.

Remembrance Sunday

———◆·◆·◆———

Christ our King make you faithful and strong to do his will, that you may reign with him in glory; and the blessing of God, Father, Son and Holy Spirit, be among you and remain with you always. Amen.

May God bless your past and remind you of his promises.
May Jesus reassure your hearts and minds of joys to come.
May the Holy Spirit fill your present with the will to trust and
serve.
And the blessing of God, who is Father, Son and Holy Spirit,
be with you always. Amen.

May the sacrifice of Christ, killed on a cross, show you the redemption that is offered to all who put their trust in him. And the blessing of God our Father, Jesus our brother and the Spirit our inspirer, be with you all. Amen.

May all victims of war and violence see that hope and justice spring eternal and can never be defeated; and so may God the Father, who named you, God the Son, who died for you, and God the Spirit, who carries you, be with you this day and for ever. Amen.

Various feast days

May the blessing of Martha's welcome;
the blessing of Mary's listening;
the blessing of action;
the blessing of reflection;
the blessing of a God who is in each of these, and in each one
   of us
be with us all.
Amen.

(Iona)

Conversion of Paul

May we never shield our eyes from the light of Christ.
May our lives be open and prepared for service.
May our hearts be converted anew every day.
And the blessing of God, Father, Son and Holy Spirit,
   enlighten each day and remain with us always. Amen.

Earl of Shaftesbury

May the eternal God bless and keep us, guard our bodies, save
our souls and bring us safe to the heavenly country, our eternal
home, where Father, Son and Holy Spirit reign, one God for
ever and ever. Amen.

Blessed Virgin Mary

Christ the Son of God, born of Mary, fill you with his grace to trust his promises and obey his will; and the blessing of God, who is Father, Son and Holy Spirit, be among you and remain with you always. Amen.

Christ the King

Christ our King make you faithful and strong to do his will, that you may reign with him in glory; and the blessing of God, Father, Son and Holy Spirit, be among you and remain with you always. Amen.

May God the Father keep you safe in his love,
May Christ the King reign in your hearts,
And the Holy Spirit inspire all you say and do.
And the blessing of God, Father, Son and Holy Spirit,
    be among you, and remain with you always. Amen.

Patronal festival

Christ, whose glory is in the heavens, fill this house and illumin-ate your hearts; and the blessing of God, Father, Son and Holy Spirit, be upon you always. Amen.

Peter

May God grant us faith to believe more deeply;
may Christ grant us compassion to forgive more readily;
may God's Holy Spirit lead us into unity and peace;
and the blessing of God, who is Father, Son and Holy Spirit,
    be upon you always. Amen.

Michael and All Angels

May the eternal God bless and keep you, guard your bodies, save your souls, direct your thoughts, and bring you safe to the heavenly country, your eternal home, where with the angels you may praise God for ever; and the blessing of God, Father, Son and Holy Spirit, be with you always. Amen.

Mary Magdalene

May the tears of Mary sharpen our senses.
May the gratitude of Mary inspire our thanks.
May the loyalty of Mary kindle our love.
And the blessing of God, Father, Son and Holy Spirit, come
    down upon us and remain with us always. Amen.

Matthew

May the Father of Mercy fill you with his love,
the Son of Righteousness assure you of his presence,
the Spirit of Truth lighten your path;
and the blessing of God, who is Father, Son and Holy Spirit,
    be upon you now and always. Amen.

Corpus Christi

May Christ always be real to you.
May you receive him with love.
And may you give his love to others.
And may God bless you,
Father, Son and Holy Spirit. Amen.

Saints' days

God give you grace to share the inheritance of his saints in glory. And the blessing of God, Father, Son and Holy Spirit, be with you now and always. Amen.

May the God of our Lord Jesus, the glorious Father, give you the Spirit of wisdom and revelation, so that you may know him better. And the blessing of God, Father, Son and Holy Spirit, be upon you always. Amen.

God, who has prepared for us a city with eternal foundations, give you grace to share the inheritance of the saints in glory; and the blessing of God, Father, Son and Holy Spirit, be among you and remain with you always. Amen.

God give you grace to follow his saints in faith and hope and love; and the blessing of God, the Father, the Son and the Holy Spirit, be among you and remain with you always. Amen.

(ASB)

SPECIAL EVENTS

School services

School leavers' blessing

1 Reach up as tall as you can
Lord God,
Bless these your children
as they grow tall and strong.
May they grow in friendship, in confidence and fun.

2 Stretch your arms wide
Lord God,
Bless these your children
as they discover your big wide world.
May they feel excited by all the new things there are to learn.

3 Wrap your arms round yourself to give yourself a hug
Lord God,
Bless these your children
that they discover that you love them.
May they be secure, knowing you are always with them.

4 Point outwards
Lord God,
Bless these your children
as they leave this school.
May they take with them happy memories
and joy in their hearts.

Blessing the school

Leavers repeat after leader
Lord God, bless this school.
Bless each teacher and each child.
Fill its classrooms with learning and laughter.
Fill its playground with friendship and care.
Lord God, as we leave, we bless this school;
we bless this school as we say our goodbyes.
Amen.

'Tall World' blessing

Jesus, friend of small people,
of bad people and lonely people,
be our friend too.
Call us and change us.
Make us more like you.
And the blessing of God Almighty,
the Father, the Son and the Holy Spirit,
be upon you and remain with you always.
Amen.

> *From 'Tall World' – an all-age service*
> *on Zacchaeus*

Funerals

May the Lord bring you his peace,
May he comfort you by his Spirit,
May he hear you when you call to him,
May he hold you close to his tender heart of compassion
And may he help you in every way through this time.
Indeed, may every tear that you shed bring you deeper healing
And may you know that *N.* is safe in God's eternal care.
And may the blessing of God, Father, Son and Holy Spirit,
    be with you always. Amen.

May the God who gave his only son, weep with you in your
    sorrow,
May the Christ who gave his life, stand beside you in your
    sadness,
May the Spirit who gives life to all live within you and bring
    you peace.
Amen.

Go then, wherever you must go.
Do those things which must be done.
Weep those tears which must be wept.
Learn to live without this dear one whom you loved.
But go in the knowledge of the God who travels with you:
God the Father with outstretched arms of love,
God the Son who enters the depths of our pain and shares
    our human story,

God the Spirit who heals our broken hearts;
and go in peace.
And the blessing of God Almighty, the Father, the Son and the
    Holy Spirit,
be among you and remain with you always. Amen.

Baptisms

May God who has brought you new life in Christ, fill your hearts and homes with his Spirit of never-ending love, and the blessing of God, Father, Son and Holy Spirit, be with you always. Amen.

May all those who are baptized this day continue their journey of faith and life filled with the Holy Spirit and divine love, and may God the Father who created you, God the Son who redeemed you and God the Spirit who sanctifies you bless you for evermore.

So may God's love which has touched our lives and brought new life continue with us as we journey in faith this day and for ever. Amen.

God be our strength and guide,
God be our hope and joy,
God be our vision and light,
God be our inspiration for our journey through life;
and the blessing of God, Father, Son and Holy Spirit, be with
us now and in our future. Amen.

Weddings

Father, as your love has drawn *N.* and *N.* together, we pray that that same love may guide, enrich and bless their lives, today and for ever. Amen.

Lord, your love sustains all things and gives meaning and joy to all those who live by trust in you. We offer to you our futures in the days and years to come, that we may be constantly renewed and refreshed by your eternal love. And so may the blessing of God, Father, Son and Holy Spirit, be on us all. Amen.

May God in his eternal love guide and lead you in the days to come. May he strengthen the love you have for each other, and may that love flow to family and friends and to all around you for the rest of your days. And the blessing of the Father who knows you, the Son who walks with you and the Spirit who comes to you be with you today and for eternity. Amen.

Departing and leaving

Leader, with all who are staying:
The Maker's blessing be yours, on your road, on your journey,
 guiding you, cherishing you.

All who are leaving today:
The Son's blessing be yours, wine and water, bread and stories,
 feeding you, challenging you.

Leader, with those staying:
The Spirit's blessing be yours, wind and fire, joy and wisdom,
 comforting you, disturbing you.

Those leaving:
The angels' blessing be yours, on your house, on your living,
 guarding you, encouraging you.

All:
**God's blessing be ours, the blessing of pilgrims, all the nights
 and days of our journey home.**

(Iona)

Leader: May God, who is present in sunrise and nightfall,
    and in all the hours between, in the crossing of the
      sea,
    guide your feet as you go.
    May God, who is with you when you sit and when
      you stand,

encompass you with love and lead you by the hand.
May God, who knows your path and the places
    where you rest,
be with you in your waiting, be your good news for
    sharing,
and lead you in the way that is everlasting.

All: **Amen.**

(Iona)

Blessing a house

This liturgy has been prepared for use in a home shortly after the arrival of the new occupant(s) or whenever it is considered pastorally appropriate. It stems from the recognition that Christ is Lord of all life, he is to be met and served in the ordinary circumstances of our daily lives and no area of our life is to be left untouched by him. The home is a place of significance for people, whether they are living alone or with others, for within it much of importance in our lives takes place, including eating, relaxing, sleeping, studying, conversation and hospitality. Christ spent the greater part of his life living and working in an ordinary dwelling in Nazareth, sanctifying all homes, and his ministry took him into the homes of diverse people.

The new occupant(s) may wish to invite a few friends, neighbours or members of their (new) church to share the occasion. It is assumed the parish priest will lead the service and suggested that others read from Scripture. It would be appropriate for some light refreshment to be shared after the service as an expression of fellowship and hospitality.

Holy water, a symbol of new life, healing and deliverance from evil, may be used. Put in a suitable vessel, it could be sprinkled in each room using a sprig of rosemary or other similar shrub.

If there are additional rooms to be blessed, other suitable prayers and readings may be used.

Provision is made for the blessing of a picture, cross or icon. Esther de Vaal commends this practice, which is common in the homes of Orthodox Christians, saying it 'can make the statement that in the interrelated spaces of our day Christ claims a place along with everything else'.

This liturgy could be used in the context of a Eucharist. The biblical readings and prayers would form the Ministry of the Word. The Ministry of the Sacrament could take place in the dining room or living room where a table had been suitably prepared with a cloth, candle(s), chalice, paten and purificator. Wine and bread would need to be available. The room in which the Ministry of the Sacrament is celebrated should be blessed after the section 'Return to the entrance'. There would follow: a Eucharistic prayer, the Lord's Prayer, the breaking of the bread, invitation to Communion, sharing of Communion, the Grace and the exchanging of the Peace.

At the entrance

Peace to this home
and to all who live in it.

If water is to be blessed, this prayer may be used as water is poured into a suitable vessel:

Living God, sanctify this water that it may be a sign of your power to dispel all evil and of the new life Christ brings to us. Through its use may this home receive your blessing. We ask this in his name. Amen.

In the kitchen

Praise the Lord and give thanks to him:
and serve him humbly and gladly.

Father, you give the fruits of your creation from all continents and climates to provide us with nourishment and enjoyment.

Bless this kitchen that all who prepare food here may do so conscious of your bountiful provision and our dependence upon the work of others. Amen.

In the dining room

Reading
Then Jesus directed them to have all the people sit down in groups on the green grass ... Taking the five loaves and the two fish and looking up to heaven, he gave thanks and broke the loaves. Then he gave them to the disciples to set before the people. He also divided the two fish among them all. They all ate and were satisfied.

(Mark 6.39–42 NIV)

Father, you provide food and drink to be a source of nourishment, pleasure and fellowship. Bless this room that all who gather here may be mindful of your goodness and grateful for your generosity. Amen.

In the sitting/living room

Reading
As Jesus and his disciples were on their way, he came to a village where a woman named Martha opened her home to him. She had a sister called Mary, who sat at the Lord's feet listening to what he said. But Martha was distracted by all the preparations that had to be made. She came to him and asked, 'Lord, don't you care that my sister has left me to do the work by myself? Tell her to help me!' 'Martha, Martha,' the Lord answered, 'you are worried and upset about many things, but

only one thing is needed. Mary has chosen what is better, and it will not be taken away from her.'

(Luke 10.38–42 NIV)

Father, your Son enjoyed the company of Martha, Mary and Lazarus at Bethany. Bless this room that it may be a place of relaxation and conversation, where relationships are strengthened, friendships renewed and lives enriched. Amen.

In a workroom/study/office

Father, your Son served as a carpenter at Nazareth, sanctifying all work. Bless this room that the gifts and time of those who work here may be employed usefully and creatively to your glory. **Amen.**

In the bedroom

Save us, O Lord, while waking, and guard us sleeping:
**that awake we may watch with Christ and asleep may rest
in peace.**

Father, may we order our lives to give time for work and worship, conversation and silence, activity and rest. Bless this bedroom that those who use it may enjoy the peace of sleep and the knowledge that they are enfolded in your love. Amen.

In a child's bedroom

Reading

At that time, the disciples came to Jesus and asked 'Who is the greatest in the kingdom of heaven?' He called a little child and had him stand among them. And he said: 'I tell you the truth, unless you change and become like little children, you will

70

never enter the kingdom of heaven. Therefore, whoever humbles himself like this child is the greatest in the kingdom of heaven. And whoever welcomes a little child like this in my name, welcomes me . . . See that you do not look down on one of these little ones. For I tell you that their angels in heaven always see the face of my Father in heaven.'

(Matthew 18.1–5, 10 NIV)

Father, we ask you to bless this room, praying that your holy angels may watch over and protect all who sleep here. Amen.

In a guest room

Reading
Jesus . . . looked up and said to him, 'Zacchaeus, come down immediately. I must stay at your house today.' So he came down at once and welcomed him gladly.

(Luke 19.5 and 6 NIV)

Father, your Son was gladly received as a guest by Zacchaeus. Bless this room that all who use it may feel welcome in this home. We ask this in the name of Jesus. Amen.

If there is more than one bedroom, this shorter prayer may be used:

Father, bless this room that those who use it may enjoy the peace of sleep and the awareness of your constant presence. Amen.

In the bathroom

I will sprinkle clean water on you:
and you will be clean.

Father, we are temples of your Holy Spirit, persons where you dwell, and your Son has taught us to love our neighbour as ourselves. Bless this bathroom that all who use it may care for their bodies and serve you faithfully. Amen.

Return to the entrance

Reading
The Lord appeared to Abraham near the great trees of Mamre while he was sitting near the entrance to his tent in the heat of the day. Abraham looked up and saw three men standing nearby. When he saw them, he hurried from the entrance of his tent to meet them and bowed low to the ground. He said, 'If I have found favour in your eyes, my Lord, do not pass your servant by. Let a little water be brought, and then you may wash your feet and rest under this tree. Let me get you something to eat, so you can be refreshed and then go on your way – now that you have come to your servant.' 'Very well,' they answered, 'we will do as you say.'

(Genesis 18.1–5 NIV)

Father, we pray that our eyes may be opened to discover that in welcoming others we are meeting you, and in offering hospitality we are serving you in friend and stranger. Amen.

In the room where refreshment is to be served

The Lord's Prayer

The Grace

The Peace may be exchanged, prefaced by a suitable invitation after the Grace.

Blessing a house

If a picture or religious object is to be blessed, it could be done when the room is reached in which it is placed. This prayer may be used:

Bless this _____ in the name of the Father, the Son and the Holy Spirit, that it may be to *N.* a constant reminder of *his/her/their* faith and the presence of Christ in our daily lives. Amen.

For healing

May the Lord's touch heal you;
may his words inspire you,
may his way give you life,
and the blessing of God, Father, Son and Holy Spirit,
   be among you, and remain with you always. Amen.

May the Lord give you strength and wisdom.
May the Lord give you his healing power.
May the Lord give you grace to fight the good fight of faith
   and win the crown of righteousness.
And the blessing of God, Father, Son and Holy Spirit, be with
   you always. Amen.

Closing prayers

Watch now, dear Lord, with those who wake or watch or weep
   tonight,
and give your angels charge over those who sleep.
Tend your sick ones, O Lord Christ,
rest your weary ones,
bless your dying ones,
soothe your suffering ones,
pity your afflicted ones,
shield your joyous ones, and all for your love's sake.
Amen.

And now may the God of hope
fill us with all joy and peace in believing
that we may abound in hope
in the power of the Holy Spirit.
Amen.

(Iona)

May the God who shakes heaven and earth,
whom death could not contain,
who lives to disturb and heal us,
bless you with power to go forth
and proclaim the gospel. Amen.

(Janet Morley, *All Desires Known*)

For reconciliation and social justice

May the God who binds up the broken-hearted,
who proclaims freedom to those held captive by poverty,
and promises to all who mourn his comfort,
bless you with beauty instead of ashes,
the oil of gladness in place of grief,
and instead of your spirit of despair,
a garment of unending praise;
through Jesus Christ our Lord.
Amen.

May the Lord God lead us from this place
and take us to where he is living;
may he lead us to a new awareness of the poor
and show us his home among them;
may he lead us to a new desire for justice
and give us a glimpse of the Kingdom he is building;
may he fill our hearts with his love and generosity
and anoint us to be bearers of good news;
may his blessing be upon us as it is upon the poor,
and may he show us what he wants us to do.
Amen.

May the blessing of the God of peace and justice be with us;
may the blessing of the Son who weeps the tears of the world's
   suffering be with us;

and may the blessing of the Spirit who inspires us to
    reconciliation and hope be with us;
from now into eternity.
Amen.

For mission

May God write a message upon your heart,
bless and direct you,
then send you out –
living letters of the Word.
Amen.

(Iona)

May the God who told us to preach the Gospel to the ends of
the earth give you boldness and courage to share the Good
News of his redeeming love. May he use you for the furtherance
of his kingdom at home, at work and in our community and
may his blessing be upon you today and always. Amen.

May the power of the Spirit of Pentecost give you strength
to proclaim, by word and action, the saving grace of God's
redeeming love, and the blessing of God, Father, Son and Holy
Spirit be with you. Amen.

General blessings

May God bestow his gift of love on you.
May he teach you how to share that love with others.
May his love lead you to everlasting life.
And may God bless you, Father, Son and Holy Spirit. Amen.

God bring you to the home that Christ prepares for all who
    love him. Amen.
God give you the will to live each day in life eternal. Amen.
God grant you the citizenship of heaven, with the blessed and
    beloved, and the whole company of the redeemed. Amen.
And the blessing of God, who is Father, Son and Holy Spirit,
    be among you and remain with you always. Amen.

The circle of Jesus keep you from sorrow
The circle of Jesus today and tomorrow
The circle of Jesus your foes confound
The circle of Jesus your life surround.

The Father on you his blessing bestow
The Son his love towards you flow
The Spirit his presence to you show
On you and all the folk you know
On you and all who around you go
The Threefold blessing may you know

The joy of this day be yours
The joy of this week be yours
The joy of this year be yours
The joy of the Father be yours
The joy of the Spirit be yours
The joy of the Son be yours
Joy for ever and ever be yours
The hands of the Father uphold you
The hands of the Saviour enfold you
The hands of the Spirit surround you
And the blessing of God Almighty
Father, Son and Holy Spirit
Uphold you evermore.

(David Adam)

May the God who created the heavens and the earth
and who knew you before you were born
continue to create his image in you.
Amen.

May the God who saw all that he had made,
'and behold it was very good',
look upon you and see in you his goodness.
Amen.

May the God who rested on the seventh day
from all his work of creation,
bring rest and refreshment to you and all the world.
Amen.

May the blessing of the one who is gracious beyond our
    imagining,
be upon you.

General blessings

May the blessing of the one who is generous beyond our
   deserving,
be within you.

May the blessing of the one whose arms are always open
be beneath you and over you and under you and around you
and everywhere you go.
Amen.

May the peace of the gentle winds inspire you,
the power of the raging storm enliven you,
the freshness of the snowy storm cleanse you,
the warmth of the summer sun comfort you;
and may every season remind you of the God who blesses
   you.

Leader: May God the Father, who created you, fulfil in you his
         heavenly purpose.
All: **Amen.**

Leader: May God the Son, who redeemed you, be always
         present with you, to guide and support you in the
         work which you do for him and his church.
All: **Amen.**

Leader: May God the Holy Spirit, who sanctifies and streng-
         thens you, fill your hearts and minds with all that
         you need to serve God faithfully.
All: **Amen.**

Leader: And the blessing of God Almighty, the Father, the
         Son and the Holy Spirit, be among you and remain
         with you always.
All: **Amen.**

Leader: Go in peace to love and serve the Lord.
All: **In the name of Christ. Amen.**

May the blessing of God go before you.
May her grace and peace abound.
May her spirit live within you.
May her love wrap you round.
May her blessing remain with you always.
May you walk on holy ground.
Amen.

May God make his light to shine in our hearts, to enlighten our lives from within, and may the blessing of God Almighty, the Father, the Son, and the Holy Spirit, abide with us always. Amen.

Aaronic blessing

The LORD bless you and keep you; the LORD make his face shine upon you and be gracious to you; the LORD turn his face towards you and give you peace.

(Numbers 6.24–26 NIV)

The Grace

The grace of our Lord Jesus Christ, the love of God, and the fellowship of the Holy Spirit be with us always. Amen.

Creator of worlds, all height and depth,
Hold you now in gentle care.
Christ, redeemer, defeating death,

Walk with you, protect from fear.
Spirit of life, sustaining breath,
Guide your journey, far and near.
Live God's presence here on earth;
Let your heart bring love to birth.
Blessings now upon you be from our God,
the one in three.

May he, who for the finishing of God's work laid down his life,
strengthen you for all the work he gives you to do, whether it is
at work, at home or in the community, and the blessing of God
Almighty, Father, Son and Holy Spirit be upon you and remain
with you always. Amen.

(Peter Cope)

May the love of God the Father surround you;
may Jesus, the Good Shepherd, walk with you;
may the joy of the Holy Spirit fill your heart with peace;
and the blessing of God Almighty, the Father, the Son, and
    the Holy Spirit,
be among you and remain with you this day and for
    evermore.

(Christopher Herbert)

May God the most holy enfold you;
may Jesus our Saviour restore you;
may the Holy Spirit surround you;
and the blessing of God Almighty, the Father, the Son, and
    the Holy Spirit,
be among you and remain with you this day and for
    evermore.

(Christopher Herbert)

God, the Holy Trinity, most wise, most loving and most
    wonderful,
give you his strength, his joy and his peace;
and the blessing of God Almighty, the Father, the Son, and
    the Holy Spirit,
be among you and remain with you this day and for
    evermore.

(Christopher Herbert)

May the Holy Shepherd guide you;
may the saints of God pray for you;
may the angels of God be with you on your way,
and the blessing of God Almighty, the Father, the Son, and
    the Holy Spirit,
be among you and remain with you this day and for
    evermore.

(Christopher Herbert)

May the love of God enfold you;
may the mercy of God absolve you;
may the strength of God support you;
may the peace of God console you;
and may the blessing of God Almighty,
Father, Son and Holy Spirit,
be with you now and evermore.
(*Frank Colquhoun, New Parish Prayers*)

May God surprise us and inspire us at every turn in our
    journeys of life.
May we encounter him in _____.
May God be with us in our going out and in our coming in.

General blessings

May God be with us in our work and in our leisure.
May God be with us in life's hills and in its valleys.
May God be with us in company and in solitude.
May God be with us in our pilgrimage and at its end.
And the blessing of God, the Father, Son and Holy Spirit,
   abide with you always.

(Stanley Pritchard)

Father, as we go forth from this service in church,
strengthen us for service in the world;
that the words we have heard and said and sung
may find expression in our daily life and work,
to the glory of your holy name.

(Frank Colquhoun, New Parish Prayers)

The blessing of the Lord rest and remain upon all his people,
   in every land, of every tongue;
the Lord meet in mercy all who seek him;
the Lord comfort all who suffer and mourn;
the Lord hasten his coming, and give us his people peace by
   all means, now and for ever.

(Handley C. G. Moule)

May God sustain us in all we do and in all our ways; may he
make us humble, just and true; may he strengthen us in the life
of faith, and in holiness and righteousness, and fill our homes
with love and peace. And may the blessing of God Almighty,
the Father, the Son, and the Holy Spirit, be with us and remain
with us always.

(Frank Colquhoun, New Parish Prayers)

Special events

Leader: God bless each of us as we travel on. In our times of need, may we find a table spread in the wilderness and companions on the road.

All: **Amen.**

(Iona)

Leader: Jesus said: 'I am with you always.'
May God the Creator bless you.
May God the Son walk with you.
May God the Spirit lead your lives with love.

All: **Amen.**

(Iona)

Leader: May the grace of Jesus Christ, the love of God,
and the communion of the Holy Spirit be with us all,
this night and always.

All: **Amen.**

(Iona)

O God, set your blessing on us as we begin *this day/our journey/a new year* together.
Confirm us in the truth by which we rightly seek to live;
Confront us with the truth from which we wrongly turn away.
We ask not for what we want, but for what you know we need,
as we offer *this day/ourselves/this year* for you and to you for ever
through Jesus Christ, our Saviour. Amen.

(Iona)

Consecration

May God keep you in all your days.
May Christ shield you in all your ways.
May the Spirit bring you healing and peace.
May God the Holy Trinity drive all darkness from you and
   pour upon you blessing and light. Amen.

Church premises etc.

Heavenly Father, we thank you for the skill of those who have crafted this lectern. May it be used to your glory as we read from Holy Scripture and proclaim the Gospel of Christ's saving power of forgiveness and love.

In the name of the Father and of the Son and of the Holy Spirit. Amen.

(Elisabeth Burke)

Lord,
Bless this church newly refurbished to your glory
And in honour of St Mark,
The first of the gospel writers.
May all who gather here in faith and in its diversity of use,
To listen to your word, celebrate your sacraments and share
   in fellowship,
Experience the presence of Christ,
Who promised to be with those gathered in his name,
For he lives and reigns with you and the Holy Spirit,
One God, forever and ever. Amen.

(Ian Brackley)

Minister: Our help is in the name of the Lord
All: **who has made heaven and earth.**

Minister: Give thanks to the Lord and call upon his name;
All: **make known his deeds among the people.**

Heavenly Father,

To your honour and glory we now dedicate this newly
refurbished chapel.

We praise and thank you for the life and witness of all who
have worshipped you here in years gone by.

We pray that this chapel may be a living memorial of that
community.

Here may you be worshipped in love and sincerity.

Here may your word be proclaimed and your sacraments
celebrated with reverence and joy.

So, Father, fill this place with your presence,

that we may meet you here and our lives be enriched and
transformed in that meeting.

We make our prayer in the name of your Son, Jesus Christ,

whose life revealed your love for us in the power of the
Holy Spirit.

Amen.

Synod

The love of the risen Lord Jesus draw us to himself, the power of the risen Lord Jesus strengthen us in his service, the joy of the risen Lord Jesus fill our hearts, giving us hope in believing; and the blessing of God, Father, Son and Holy Spirit, be upon us always. Amen.

Pet services

God the Father, who creates all things,
God the Son, who redeems all things,
and God the Holy Spirit, who gives life to all things,
Bless these animals and our relationships with them.
Fill our hearts with life and love and laughter and send us on
   our way rejoicing,
and the blessing of the one true God be upon us,
our homes and our families today and always. Amen.

Dedications

May God keep you in all your days.
May Christ shield you in all your ways.
May the Spirit bring you healing and peace.
May God the Holy Trinity drive all darkness from you and
    pour upon you blessing and light. Amen.

Loving God,
bless all those who are gathered here,
that they may be a blessing to others
through Jesus Christ, our Lord. Amen.

Take us, we pray,
O Lord of our life,
firmly into your keeping;
and may the blessing of God,
Father, Son and Holy Spirit,
be upon us, now and always. Amen.

God give you more than you can ever think or ask,
God use you far beyond the challenge of your task,
God lead you further than the vision you can see,
God mould you day by day more perfectly,
God bless you, in the way he sees as best,
God bless you, that each life you touch may be blessed. Amen.

Be held in the stillness of God
and may that stillness
bless and keep you
this night and always. Amen.

Ever-living God,
we entrust the past to your mercy,
the present to your love,
and the future to your care;
and may your blessing be upon us now and for ever. Amen.

The light of God surround you,
the love of God enfold you,
the power of God protect you,
the presence of God watch over you;
and the blessing of God, Father, Son and Holy Spirit, be upon
    you, now and for evermore. Amen.

May the power of God free your Spirit to accept his call to
    new life.
May you know each day the depth of Christ's love and respect
    for you.
May the Spirit fill you with the desire to be made new.
May the blessing of God, Father, Son and Holy Spirit, be with
    you now and for ever. Amen.

A SELECTION OF BIBLICAL BLESSINGS, EXHORTATIONS, ASCRIPTIONS, DOXOLOGIES ETC., TO DRAW WORSHIP TO A CLOSE

May the LORD whom we obey send his angel with you and give you success.

(adapted from Genesis 24.40 NIV)

The LORD bless you and keep you; the LORD make his face shine upon you and be gracious to you; the LORD turn his face towards you and give you peace.

(Numbers 6.24–26 NIV)

May the LORD our God be with us as he was with our fathers; may he never leave us nor forsake us. May he turn our hearts to him, to walk in all his ways and to keep the commands he gave us. And may the words which we have prayed before the LORD, be near to the LORD our God day and night, that he may uphold the cause of his servants according to each day's need; and may all the peoples of the earth know that the LORD is God and that there is no other.

(adapted from 1 Kings 8.57–60 NIV)

Praise be to you, O LORD, God of our father Israel, from everlasting to everlasting. Yours, O LORD, is the greatness and the power and the glory and the majesty and the splendour, for everything in heaven and earth is yours. Yours, O LORD, is the kingdom; you are exalted as head over all. Wealth and honour come from you; you are the ruler of all things. In your hands are strength and power to exalt and give strength to all. Now, our God, we give you thanks, and praise your glorious name.

(1 Chronicles 29.10–13 NIV)

Blessed be your glorious name, and may it be exalted above all blessing and praise. You alone are the LORD. You made the heavens, even the highest heavens, and all their starry host, the earth and all that is on it, the seas and all that is in them. You give life to everything, and the multitudes of heaven worship you.

(Nehemiah 9.5–6 NIV)

May the LORD answer you when you are in distress; may the name of the God of Jacob protect you. May he send you help from the sanctuary and grant you support from Zion. May he remember all your sacrifices and accept your burnt offerings. May he give you the desire of your heart and make all your plans succeed.

(Psalm 20.1–4 NIV)

We wait in hope for the LORD; he is our help and our shield. In him our hearts rejoice, for we trust in his holy name. May your unfailing love rest upon us, O LORD, even as we put our hope in you.

(Psalm 33.20–22 NIV)

May the LORD show you his constant love during the day. Each evening may you have a song and a prayer to the God of your life.

May the LORD send you his light and his truth, and lead you; may he bring you back here to worship him anew.

(*adapted from* Psalms 42.8 and 43.3 GNB)

Praise be to the LORD God, the God of Israel, who alone does marvellous deeds. Praise be to his glorious name for ever; may the whole earth be filled with his glory. Amen and Amen.

(Psalm 72.18–19 NIV)

May the LORD teach you to number your days, and apply your heart to wisdom. May he satisfy you each morning with his constant love, that all your days you may rejoice and sing. May your Master show you his mighty deeds, and let your children see his glory. May the gracious favour of the LORD your God be upon you, and prosper the work of your hands.

(*adapted from* Psalm 90.12, 16–17 NIV)

May the LORD answer you when you call upon him and strengthen you with his strength. When you are surrounded by troubles, may the LORD keep you safe. May he save you from your enemies by his power. May he fulfil his promises in you. May he complete the work that he has begun in you.

(*adapted from* Psalm 138.3, 7, 8 GNB)

May the Spirit of the LORD rest upon you: the Spirit of wisdom and of understanding; the Spirit of counsel and of power; the Spirit of knowledge and of the fear of the LORD. And may you delight in the fear of the LORD.

(*adapted from* Isaiah 11.2–3 NIV)

The LORD look upon you and heal you; the LORD guide you and restore comfort to you; the LORD bring praise to your lips and give peace, to those far and near. Amen.

(*adapted from* Isaiah 57.18–19 NIV)

I praise you, Father, Lord of heaven and earth, because you have hidden these things from the wise and learned, and revealed them to little children. Yes, Father, for this was your good pleasure.

(Matthew 11.25–26 NIV)

Now I commend you to God and to the word of his grace, which is able to build you up, and give you an inheritance among all the saints.

(*adapted from* Acts 20.32, RSV)

Oh, the depth of the riches of the wisdom and knowledge of God! How unsearchable his judgments, and his paths beyond tracing out! Who has known the mind of the Lord? Or who has been his counsellor? Who has ever given to God, that God should repay him? For from him and through him and to him are all things. To him be the glory for ever! Amen.

(Romans 11.33–36 NIV)

Therefore I urge you, brothers and sisters, in view of God's mercy, to offer your bodies as living sacrifices, holy and pleasing to God – this is your spiritual act of worship. Do not conform any longer to the pattern of this world, but be transformed by the renewing of your mind. Then you will be able to test and approve what God's will is – his good, pleasing and perfect will.

(Romans 12.1–2 NIV)

May the God who gives endurance and encouragement give you a spirit of unity among yourselves as you follow Christ Jesus, so that with one heart and mouth you may glorify the God and Father of our Lord Jesus Christ.

(Romans 15.5–6 NIV)

May the God of hope fill you with all joy and peace as you trust in him, so that you may overflow with hope by the power of the Holy Spirit.

(Romans 15.13 NIV)

Let us give glory to God! He is able to make you stand firm in your faith, according to the Good News I preach about Jesus Christ and according to the revelation of the secret truth which was hidden for long ages in the past. Now, however, that truth has been brought out into the open through the writings of the prophets; and by the command of the eternal God it is made known to all nations, so that all may believe and obey. To the only God, who alone is all-wise, be glory through Jesus Christ for ever! Amen.

(Romans 16.25–27 GNB)

Thanks be to God! He gives us the victory through our Lord Jesus Christ. Therefore, my dear brothers and sisters, stand firm. Let nothing move you. Always give yourselves fully to the work of the Lord, because you know that your labour in the Lord is not in vain.

(1 Corinthians 15.57–58 NIV)

Finally, brothers and sisters, good-bye. Aim for perfection, listen to my appeal, be of one mind, live in peace. And the God of love and peace will be with you.

(2 Corinthians 13.11 NIV)

May the grace of the Lord Jesus Christ, and the love of God, and the fellowship of the Holy Spirit be with you all.

(2 Corinthians 13.14 NIV)

Grace and peace to you from God our Father and the Lord Jesus Christ, who gave himself for our sins to rescue us from the present evil age, according to the will of our God and Father, to whom be glory for ever and ever. Amen.

(Galatians 1.3–5 NIV)

Let us not become weary in doing good, for at the proper time we will reap a harvest if we do not give up. Therefore, as we have opportunity, let us do good to all people, especially to those who belong to the family of believers.

(Galatians 6.9–10 NIV)

Praise be to the God and Father of our Lord Jesus Christ, who has blessed us in the heavenly realms with every spiritual blessing in Christ.

(Ephesians 1.3 NIV)

Now to him who is able to do immeasurably more than all we ask or imagine, according to his power that is at work within us, to him be glory in the church and in Christ Jesus throughout all generations, for ever and ever! Amen.

(Ephesians 3.20–21 NIV)

May God the Father and the Lord Jesus Christ give to all Christian brothers and sisters peace and love with faith. May God's grace be with all those who love our Lord Jesus Christ with undying love.

(Ephesians 6.23–24 GNB)

Rejoice in the Lord always. I will say it again: Rejoice! Let your gentleness be evident to all. The Lord is near. Do not be anxious about anything, but in everything, by prayer and petition, with thanksgiving, present your requests to God. And the peace of God, which transcends all understanding, will guard your hearts and minds in Christ Jesus.

(Philippians 4.4–7 NIV)

Finally, brothers and sisters, whatever is true, whatever is noble, whatever is right, whatever is pure, whatever is lovely, whatever is admirable – if anything is excellent or praiseworthy – think about such things . . . And the God of peace will be with you.

(Philippians 4.8, 9 NIV)

Live a life worthy of the Lord, and please him in every way. Bear fruit in every good work; grow in the knowledge of God; be strengthened with all power according to his glorious might, so that you may have great endurance and patience. Joyfully give thanks to the Father, who has qualified you to share in the inheritance of the saints in the kingdom of light.

(*based on* Colossians 1.10–12 NIV)

Let the peace of Christ rule in your hearts, since as members of one body you were called to peace. And be thankful. Let the word of Christ dwell in you richly . . . And whatever you do, whether in word or deed, do it all in the name of the Lord Jesus, giving thanks to God the Father through him.

(Colossians 3.15, 16, 17 NIV)

May the Lord make your love increase and overflow for each other and for everyone else, just as ours does for you. May he strengthen your hearts so that you will be blameless and holy in the presence of our God and Father when our Lord Jesus comes with all his holy ones.

(1 Thessalonians 3.12–13 NIV)

Be joyful always; pray continually; give thanks in all circum-stances, for this is God's will for you in Christ Jesus.

(1 Thessalonians 5.16–18 NIV)

May God himself, the God of peace, sanctify you through and through. May your whole spirit, soul and body be kept blameless at the coming of our Lord Jesus Christ. The one who calls you is faithful, and he will do it.

(1 Thessalonians 5.23–24 NIV)

May our Lord Jesus Christ himself and God our Father, who loved us and by his grace gave us eternal encouragement and good hope, encourage your hearts and strengthen you in every good deed and word.

(2 Thessalonians 2.16–17 NIV)

The Lord is faithful, and he will strengthen and protect you from the evil one. We have confidence in the Lord that you are doing and will continue to do the things we command. May the Lord direct your hearts into God's love and Christ's perseverance.

(2 Thessalonians 3.3–5 NIV)

Now may the Lord of peace himself give you peace at all times and in every way. The Lord be with all of you.

(2 Thessalonians 3.16 NIV)

So let us praise God, the blessed and only Ruler, the King of kings and Lord of lords. He alone is immortal, and he lives in unapproachable light, whom no-one has seen or can see. To him be honour and might for ever. Amen.

(*based on* 1 Timothy 6.15–16 NIV)

If you are wealthy, don't be proud: wealth is easily lost – so don't put your confidence in that! Have faith in God, who is rich and blesses us with everything we need to enjoy life. Do as much good as you can; help everyone. Be generous, and share what you have. In this way you will store up for yourselves a treasure which will be a solid foundation for the future. And then you will know what real life is like!

(adapted from 1 Timothy 6.17–19 NIV)

May the God of peace, who through the blood of the eternal covenant brought back from the dead our Lord Jesus, that great shepherd of the sheep, equip you with everything good for doing his will, and may he work in us what is pleasing to him, through Jesus Christ, to whom be glory for ever and ever. Amen.

(Hebrews 13.20–21 NIV)

The God of all grace, who called you to his eternal glory in Christ, after you have suffered a little while, will himself restore you and make you strong, firm and steadfast. To him be the power for ever and ever. Amen.

(1 Peter 5.10–11 NIV)

Grow in the grace and knowledge of our Lord and Saviour Jesus Christ. To him be glory both now and for ever! Amen.

(2 Peter 3.18 NIV)

To those who have been called, who are loved by God the Father and kept by Jesus Christ: mercy, peace and love be yours in abundance.

(Jude verses 1–2 NIV)

To him who is able to keep you from falling, and to present you before his glorious presence without fault and with great joy – to the only God our Saviour be glory, majesty, power and authority, through Jesus Christ our Lord, before all ages, now and for evermore! Amen.

(Jude verses 24–25 NIV)

Grace and peace to you from him who is, and who was, and who is to come, and from the seven spirits before his throne, and from Jesus Christ, who is the faithful witness, the firstborn from the dead, and the ruler of the kings of the earth.

To him who loves us and has freed us from our sins by his blood, and has made us to be a kingdom and priests to serve his God and Father – to him be glory and power for ever and ever! Amen.

(Revelation 1.4–6 NIV)

To him who sits on the throne and to the Lamb be praise and honour and glory and power, for ever and ever!

(Revelation 5.13 NIV)

Amen! Praise and glory and wisdom and thanks and honour and power and strength be to our God for ever and ever. Amen!

(Revelation 7.12 NIV)

The kingdom of the world has become the kingdom of our Lord and of his Christ, and he will reign for ever and ever.

(Revelation 11.15 NIV)

We give thanks to you, Lord God Almighty, you who are and who were, because you have taken your great power and have begun to reign.

(*adapted from* Revelation 11.17 NIV)

Now have come the salvation and the power and the kingdom of our God, and the authority of his Christ. For the accuser of our brothers and sisters . . . has been hurled down . . . Therefore rejoice, you heavens and you who dwell in them!

(Revelation 12.10, 12 NIV)

Great and marvellous are your deeds, Lord God Almighty. Just and true are your ways, King of the ages. Who will not fear you, O Lord, and bring glory to your name? For you alone are holy. All nations will come and worship before you, for your righteous acts have been revealed.

(Revelation 15.3–4 NIV)

Hallelujah! For our Lord God Almighty reigns. Let us rejoice and be glad and give him glory!

(Revelation 19.6b–7a NIV)